Mixed Good Continua
and Public Policy

Stephen Shmanske

Economics Paper 2
ABS 1999:2

A previous version of this Paper was presented in the Economics Workshop at California State University, Hayward. This paper is a further refinement and extension of arguments made in Public Goods, Mixed Goods and Monopolistic Competition, Texas A&M University Press, 1991.

Discussion Paper Series

This discussion paper series is issued by The Centre for International Business and Economic Research (CIBER) on behalf of Anglia Business School.

CIBER was established in 1998 as a University Designated Research Centre within the Business School with the aim of fostering interdisciplinary research in the areas of international business and economics.

All papers submitted are subject to a refereeing process. All views expressed are those of the authors and not necessarily those of CIBER. The discussion papers often represent preliminary or developing work, which is circulated to facilitate discussion and comment.

Aims of the Series

- Promote the dissemination of Business School research within the institution and through the wider research community;

- Further promote the research profile and ethos of the Business School;

- Promote a greater awareness of the wide range of research specialisms within the Business School, leading to a cross-fertilisation of ideas and greater evolution of team research;

- Provide a mechanism for the discussion, review and development of research ideas.

Editors of Discussion Paper Series

Stephen Ison and Paul Saw
CIBER
Anglia Business School

Series Secretary
For further information about this and other Discussion Papers in the series, please contact:

Barbara Mornin
CIBER
Anglia Business School
Anglia Polytechnic University
East Road
Cambridge
UK
CB1 1PT

Tel: 01223 363271
Fax: 01223 352900
E-mail: bmlbm@bridge.anglia.ac.uk

Author Profile
Stephen Shmanske is a Professor of Economics at California State University, Hayward where he has been on the faculty since receiving his Ph.D. at U.C.L.A. He has also been a visiting professor at Anglia Polytechnic University in Cambridge, England. His research interests include transportation economics, the economics of sports, the economics of price discrimination, public finance, and applied microeconomic theory. His research has resulted in a book on public goods and dozens of articles published in a wide range of academic journals. He is also a member of the advisory board for the Smith Center for Private Enterprise Studies on the Cal State campus.

Address for correspondence:
Department of Economics
California State University, Hayward
Hayward, CA 94542

Tel: 510-528-0506   Fax: 510-885-4699
E-mail: sshmansk@csuhayward.edu

Comments with respect to this paper would be most welcome and should be addressed to the author.

First published February 1999

Chlorine free paper.

ISBN   1-900-432-03-X

Published by:

Earlybrave

PUBLICATIONS LIMITED

PO Box No. 3165
Brentwood
Essex CM13 1TL
Telephone: 01277 260436

Further copies available from the publisher.

Mixed Good Continua and Public Policy

Abstract

Pure public goods and pure private goods are sometimes seen as polar opposite cases enclosing a range of mixed goods. Since there is some controversy over the proper definition of a public good, there is a related ambiguity over what constitutes a mixed good. This paper explores the many different attributes that have been connected with public goods and derives the corresponding nature of the mixed good continuum for each case. Whether interventionist or free market policies are implied depends on the nature of the attribute defining the pure public good and on the method of developing the mixed good continuum between the polar cases.

Introduction

The debate over whether public (collective) goods lead to a rationale for government intervention into the economy is likely to continue endlessly. At least part of the reason is that no one definition of public goods has gained universal acceptance. If economists cannot agree on what is meant by the term, public goods, then their policy conclusions are likely to reflect that disagreement. The depth of the disagreement is evidenced even in the distilled treatment of public goods that intermediate textbooks offer. Indeed, out of a sample of fourteen intermediate microeconomic theory textbooks, six different views are offered.[1] The point of this paper, however, is not to argue that one definition should be adopted over the others. Rather, the thrust here is to illustrate how one's policy conclusions are influenced by one's choice and use of definitions.[2] A brief example may serve to illustrate this point. If public goods are defined to be those goods for which consumption is non-excludable, then government provision may be the only way to produce such a good. While even this point can be contested, probably most economists would agree that a rationale exists for government intervention in the case of such "pure" public goods. Alternatively, however, if non-rival consumption is the distinguishing feature, then as the various models of "excludable public goods" make clear, no clear rationale exists for intervention.[3]

This paper is actually concerned with different definitions of mixed goods, that somewhat nebulous range of possibilities flanked by pure private goods and pure public goods. Although the pure public good case was of paramount interest originally as a stark contrast to the traditional private goods models, the pure cases, private and public, were soon seen to be too restrictive to encompass all of the possibilities. Some sort of mixed good was needed to fill the middle ground.

In fleshing out the middle ground of mixed goods, two aspects deserve our attention. First, the characteristics defining the pure polar cases need to be addressed. Second, the method of combining the public good characteristics with the private good characteristics needs to be examined. The first issue was highlighted above by the contrast between the non-excludable and non-rival aspects of public goods. The second issue can be highlighted with the following example. For the moment suppose we believe that there is a rationale for government intervention in the case of pure public goods, but that a free market policy is optimal in the case of private goods. What can we say about mixed goods? Do we build up from private goods, thus concentrating on how the market mechanism that works so well in the private goods case will also be operative in the mixed goods case? Or do we analogize down from pure public goods, noting that some of the elements alleged to cause market failure in the pure public good case also exist for mixed goods? Both of these approaches have been utilized. For example, consider Demsetz [1970] who argues that the logic employed in the private goods analysis of joint supply can be extended to apply to public goods, thus yielding optimal private sector public good provision. Alternatively, consider Samuelson who, after rejecting the view that the world is composed solely of pure public goods and pure private goods, states that we are left, "with a knife-edge pole of the private-good case, and with all the rest of the world in the public-good domain by virtue of involving some 'consumption externality'."[4]   It is clear to Samuelson that government intervention may be required most of the time.

Table I lists several alternative views of the distinguishing feature that differentiates public goods from private goods. These views are neither mutually exclusive, nor independent. Indeed, some of the views are subsets or derivatives of other views. Others, like non-rivalry and non-excludability can exist separately or in conjunction. The only claim is that the highlighted feature has been used to contrast public goods and private goods. Many of the viewpoints have an associated middle range of mixed goods. The body of this paper, Section III, examines each of these views in turn. First, however, I introduce the two main features that have been used to distinguish public and private goods.

Rivalry and Excludability

Many of the distinctions being stressed in the table are derivative of two basic issues, non-excludability and non-rivalry. Here, a brief introduction serves to set the stage. A synthesizing discussion will be saved for later.

Non-rivalry refers to the case where one person's consumption of the good does not "use up" the good, so that it can still be "consumed" by others. A non-rival good, like national defense, can be consumed by all, whereas a rival good, like an apple, once consumed by one person, is gone. Section III shows how non-rivalry leads to many of the issues, such as zero marginal cost, no crowding, and vertical summations of demand curves, that are listed in Table I.

Non-excludability, refers to the ability of the consumer to consume whatever amount is produced without having to pay for it. Again, national defense is often used as an example. Once it is produced, everyone can consume it without paying. Alternatively, to consume an excludable good, an individual may have to pay the seller for it. The ability to exclude non-payers allows the producer to charge a price and recoup the production cost.

Alternatively, the ability to consume without paying leads to the free rider problem. Non-excludability becomes an issue when externalities and quantity choice are examined as in 3 and 7.

The use of national defense as a prototypical example of a public good is misleading because it simultaneously illustrates non-rivalry and non-excludability.[5] Perhaps because of this, the most frequent definition of a public good employed by the textbooks listed in footnote 1 includes both non-rivalry and non-excludability. Alternatively, a private good, like an apple, is excludable and rival. This approach tends to mislead because the two aspects of non-excludability and non-rivalry are not necessarily linked as they are in the example of national defense. They can appear individually. That non-rivalry can exist with exclusion has been noted, as the models of excludable public goods referenced in footnote 3 illustrate. An extended discussion of this issue is presented by Laux-Meiselbach [1988] who uses a two- by-two matrix to examine the full taxonomy of possibilities with respect to the separable issues of excludability and rivalry.

Furthermore, the issues of excludability and rivalry should be kept separate because they lead to different lines of argument - non-rivalry to a distinction in the theoretical analytics between public and private, and non-excludability to the free rider problem. These and other issues are addressed further in the next section.

Mixed Good Continua

There is no obviously straightforward order in which to consider the thirteen different possibilities in Table I. Some of the views stem directly from non-rivalry, and some are further refinements of these. This alone would be straightforward enough, but at the same time various aspects of non-excludability are woven into the argument. Meanwhile,, some of the views seem to start out as combinations of non-rivalry and non-excludability but, upon closer inspection, only one or the other of these factors is operative. Furthermore, still other views seem to defy categorization.

I have chosen to place the direct discussions of rivalry and excludability near the bottom of the list. In this way I can use the discussions of rivalry and excludability to summarize the different implications of these aspects in the various other continua.

The first two distinctions in Table I are somewhat different than the rest in that they focus directly on the positive and normative aspects of whether a good is produced privately or publicly and only indirectly on the aspects of the good in question that cause its placement in one sector or the other. Distinctions 3-8 stem mostly from some technical aspects in the analysis of the non-rival property, but issues of excludability seep in. Distinction 9 follows next because it has issues of both non-rivalry and non-excludability. Distinction 10, on excludability, can now tie up some themes from 3-9. Distinction 11 again covers issues of non-rivalry and, given the possibility of exclusion, the desirability of exclusion and leads directly to the two dimensional approach in 12. Finally, in 13, a revisiting of non-rivalry ties things together.

Public good	Mixed Good	Private Good
1. actually produced and demanded in the public sector	regulated, taxed or subsidized	actually produced and demanded in the private sector
2. should always be produced publicly	module of production depends on social welfare function	should always be produced privately
3. no quantity choice for consumer		quality adjustment by consumer
4. same argument in each individual's utility function	same argument in utility functions of subset of all consumers	different argument in each individual's utility function
5. vertical summation of individual demand curves	both? neither?	horizontal summation of individual demand curves
6. all consumers share the good	partial subset of consumers share	only one consumer uses the good
7. $U = u_i$	$U^{-p} = \sum (u_i)^{-p}$	$U = \sum u_i$
8. no crowding	crowding after too much use	absolute crowding after one consumer
9. severe consumption or production externalities	partial externalities	no externalities
10. no exclusion	partial exclusion	costless exclusion
11. zero marginal cost for extra consumption		positive marginal cost for extra consumption
12. utilization dimension disappears	both dimensions are relevant	public dimension disappears
13. non-rivalry in consumption		rivalry in consumption

Table I: Viewpoints On Pure Public, Pure Private, And Mixed Goods

1.The first distinction is based on whether the good is produced in the public sector or the private sector. As a purely definitional matter, we could distinguish private goods, that is, those produced is completely decentralized markets, from public goods, that is, those produced under complete socialism. The middle range would include regulated production, and subsidized or taxed production.

On the surface, this approach pays little attention to why a good is produced in or demanded by one sector or the other. It is a purely positive, descriptive division of the way things are. As such, this first classification begs the question that the other viewpoints are trying to answer. I include it here because some, perhaps those who are not formally within the economics field, will use the terms public and private goods merely to identify whether (but not why) the good is produced publicly or privately.

The concentration of demand and production in this first view actually permits a further subdivision of public versus private provision. That is, we could distinguish between production and consumption because these need not be in the same sector.

Collinge [1985] for example, discusses decentralized contracting schemes as applied to both public and private goods. Indeed, nuclear warheads are demanded by the public sector but produced in the private sector, while education is demanded privately (and also possibly publicly) but produced publicly (and also privately). Neither warheads nor education would be purely public or private according to this viewpoint. Notwithstanding this subdivision, we still have only a definitional distinction and not a causal explanation.

2. Usually the choice between public and private production takes on a normative aspect. Given some goal, should a good be produced publicly or privately? The answer might depend on the nature of exclusion costs, the possibility of free riding, the distribution of income, differences in production costs or a host of other criteria which are addressed below. Of general interest, however, is the viewpoint expounded by John Head and Carl Shoup [1969]. Head and Shoup argue that a pure public good is one in which a "non-marketing mode" always leads to higher social welfare. By "non-marketing mode" Head and Shoup essentially mean bureaucratic or administrative decision making using some demand revealing process and forced taxation. Alternatively, pure private goods are those for which the

"marketing mode" leads to higher social welfare. The "marketing mode" is essentially voluntary exchange activity. The middle ground of "ambiguous goods" are those for which some social welfare functions indicate that the non-marketing mode leads to higher utility while other social welfare functions indicate that the marketing mode should be used. The turning point for ambiguous goods revolves around the ability to redistribute income in a non-marketing mode through tax policy.

Upon further inspection, all goods must be ambiguous under this classification. For example a libertarian's concept of the social welfare function would not allow forced taxation in any case thus always favoring the marketing mode. Meanwhile, a socialist's view might place all importance on equality, essentially disallowing any voluntary activity that would bestow unequal benefits, and squarely placing all production in the non-marketing mode. The inability to ever agree on a social welfare function makes this distinction vacuous for policy prescription.

3. Robert Staaf [1983] considers a good which might be produced either as a public good or a private good. Produced as a private good, each consumer could consume it until his marginal rate of substitution (MRS) equaled his price. Produced as a public good, each consumer must consume the same amount. The public good formulation basically adds an extra constraint, that all must consume the identical amount, consequently, utilities are not as high in the public good formulation.[6] However, the private formulation might have higher costs than the public formulation, because of an added cost of exclusion.[7] Therefore, the conclusion as to where utilities are higher is ambiguous. Note that the ambiguity here depends on exclusion costs and is different from the ambiguity that Head and Shoup derived from social welfare functions.

According to Staaf, to privatize the originally non-excludable public good requires an extra cost to make the good excludable. The result of privatization is that the consumer gets to adjust quantity for the private good where he had not been able to do so for the public good. Staaf focuses on this quantity adjustment issue.

In highlighting the quantity adjustment issue as a feature that distinguishes between public and private goods, there does not seem to be a relevant middle ground. You can either adjust quantity or you can not.

However, once the economic costs of quantity adjustment are considered, the distinction between public and private pales. The possibility that the distinction rests nicely on the cost of quantity adjustment, (i.e. zero quantity adjustment cost equals private good; infinite quantity adjustment cost equals public good; and, positive, finite quantity adjustment cost equals mixed good) is not particularly fruitful. Quantity adjustment will always be costly, even for private goods, except for a free good. Neither will quantity adjustment ever be proscribed by infinite cost. An individual always has the option of producing his own public good, thereby adjusting quantity, while others possibly free ride.[8]

The possibility that individuals can produce their own public goods and thereby adjust quantity seems to have been ignored by Staaf. If we literally accept the distinction based on the possibility of adjustment, then all goods must be private.

The distinction might be saved by interpreting quantity adjustment relatively rather than absolutely. That is, because of self-production, individuals can always (at finite cost) adjust quantity absolutely, but if the good is non-rival and non-excludable, individuals can-not adjust quantity relative to others.

In this light, the characteristic of public goods is that there is no independent quantity choice for the consumer while for private goods there is. Obviously, however, this characteristic is a derivative of the more basic notions of non-rivalry and non-excludability. Just as obvious, there is no mixed good possibility surrounding quantity choice by the consumer. The consumer can either adjust quantity independently or he cannot. Curiously, there does not seem to be a mixed goods case in Staaf's analysis.

4. When asked to illustrate the use of mathematics in economics, Samuelson [1954] came up with a notationally motivated distinction between private and public goods. The distinction, based on whether the consumption of a good enters one or more person's utility function(s), leads to the well known difference in the marginal conditions describing optimality. When a good enters identically into everyone's utility function, the summation of MRSs must be compared to the marginal cost of its production. Private goods enter only one person's utility function, so only one person's MRS is compared to marginal cost.

There are two possible ways to address the related continuum between the polar endpoints in this case. The first involves notationally sliding all goods to one or the other of the poles. That is, all goods could be notationally defined as public, or likewise, all goods could be defined as private. The second possible middle ground involves a good that enters into utility functions of more than one but not all of the individuals. We shall treat these two possibilities in turn.

The first point was recognized early by both Samuelson [1958] and Buchanan [1968]. According to this argument, all goods, including pure private goods, can be defined as public goods. That is, "my consumption of bread" could enter into each person's utility function. If one does this, the marginal conditions will show a summation of MRSs for "my consumption of bread" with only one positive term and a string of zeros. According to this view, the public good case seems the more general, with the pure private good being a mathematically degenerate special case. This point of view predisposes the analyst to look for reasons why one person's private good consumption might be related to a nonzero MRS in another individual. Benevolence and paternalism come to mind. The link between public or mixed goods and externalities follows closely on the heels of this recognition.

Deeper reflection also indicates that all goods could be defined as private goods. Even for national defense we could define your consumption of national defense and my consumption of national defense as separate goods. Due to the joint production costs, the marginal conditions will evidence a multitude of corner solutions because of the discontinuous nature of marginal costs. That is, the marginal cost for more national defense for me will be zero up to a certain amount, (if the national defense has been produced for someone else), and then will suddenly become positive. If my MRS is between zero and this positive amount, then we get a corner solution for my equilibrium. There may be many different levels of national defense production for which these corner solutions hold. Mathematically, we would have to choose among these multiple solutions on the basis of the total conditions. The mathematics would be easier if we recognized that because of the joint production costs there is an implied constraint of equality between your consumption and my consumption in each of the solutions. Incorporating this constraint into the marginal equalities yields the familiar form in terms of a summation of MRSs equal to a marginal cost.

There is more than a verbal splitting of hairs going on here. When all goods are defined as public goods, my consumption of my bread and your "consumption" of my bread are equal by definition, although many of the associated MRSs are trivially equal to zero. When all goods are defined as private goods, your consumption and my consumption are unequal in general, but may be equal in equilibrium due to jointness on the production side. The trivial string of zeros in the marginal equalities for a rival good when all goods are defined as public is the counterpart of the implicit equality constraint for the case of a non-rival good when all goods are defined as private. Mathematically, neither view seems more relevant but there are important connotations associated with choosing one over the other. The private good view will focus one's attention on joint costs and joint supply and the corresponding pricing and marketing arrangements that will develop spontaneously.

The public view will focus one's attention on consumption externalities and the corresponding intervention that may be appropriate. Demsetz [1970] and Samuelson may be taken as examples of, respectively, the joint supply view and the externalities view. Illustrative of the thesis in this paper, their views of the distinction between public and private differ and, correspondingly, so do their policy recommendations.

The second possible middle ground for this characterization covers the possibility that a good enters identically into utility functions for only a subset of consumers. The difference in the marginal conditions is easily derived. A summation of MRSs taken over only the relevant subset of consumers must be compared to marginal cost.

Unfortunately, there is nothing in the notation to tell us why a particular good will be consumed by just one consumer, a subset of consumers or all of the consumers. The notational difference appears to be symptomatic of the distinction among public goods, private goods and mixed goods, but is not the cause of the distinction. Nevertheless, the power of this notation is evident. Whatever the cause of the distinction in the other formulations, the pure polar cases make use of this notation.

5. The difference in the algebraic treatment introduced by Samuelson led to a diagrammatic distinction between public and private based on whether demand curves are to be summed horizontally or vertically. The middle ground in this case is intriguing. Is some other summation besides

vertical or horizontal relevant? Perhaps some combination of vertical and horizontal summation is necessary. Interestingly, both Evans [1970] and Head [1976] argue that, because of externalities (see 9), a vertical summation followed by a horizontal summation yields the correct analysis. Alternatively (see 12), Shmanske [1982] argues that, because of joint costs in a quality dimension, a horizontal summation in one dimension should be followed by a vertical summation in another dimension. Vertical summations are symptomatic of some non-rival or joint consumption where marginal values of more than one person must be considered. Meanwhile, horizontal summations are symptomatic of rival consumption. The policy issue revolves around whether the market's spontaneous exchange and pricing mechanism, employed to ration in the rival/horizontal dimension, simultaneously accounts for the effects in the non-rival/vertical dimension. On the one hand, Evans and Head would argue that, because of externalities it does not - although Coase [1960] would disagree. On the other hand, Shmanske argues that with price discrimination, pricing in the rival dimension can capture the valuations in the non-rival dimension. Again we see that the decision of which of the public or private to highlight (in this case the vertical summation or the horizontal), affects one's conclusions for policy.

6. The theory of clubs, as originally expounded by James Buchanan [1965], considers the size of the group that shares some good in common. This viewpoint provides one motivation for the notational distinction between public and private goods given above in 4. For clubs, all members consume the same good so all member's MRSs count in the comparison of cost and benefit. Nonmembers, however, are ignored. The size of the sharing group can be: one, for a private good; the whole community, for a public good; or any size in between.

The theory of clubs gives a nice breakdown of goods as public, private or mixed but begs the question of what determines the size of the sharing group. It could be exclusion costs, congestion costs, limits on the possibility for reciprocal externalities, or one of the other viewpoints enumerated here that lead to different club sizes. Nevertheless, the theory of clubs is not without policy impact. The main impact of this theory comes from the dramatic illustration of private attempts to produce mixed goods. Indeed, many clubs are purely voluntary arrangements through which the joint costs are shared and the free rider problem is overcome. Although private production of the mixed good may not be optimal in a simplistic Paretian sense, production will certainly not be zero. Indeed, the thrust of the theory of clubs is clearly on voluntary attempts in the private sector to produce the mixed good as opposed to public sector attempts to decide the extent of sharing and the incidence of taxation.

7. Jan Tinbergen [1984] attempts to capture the continuum of public to private with an algebraic expression involving one parameter. For private goods, the total production U is the summation of each individual's consumption, ui while for public goods, total production and individual consumption are related by equality. The expression given in Table I for the mixed good case reduces to the private good case when p equals negative one. Alternatively, as p approaches negative infinity, the expression approaches the public good case.

Tinbergen is attempting to get at a mathematical representation of partial rivalry measured in consumption units of the good. For public goods, given a fixed amount of production, one person's consumption does not reduce anyone else's. For private goods, however, with the same fixed production, one person's consumption must reduce someone else's on a one-for-one basis. In Tinbergen's mixed good range, one person's consumption decreases someone else's but by less than the increase to the first person. Congestion might be one example of this phenomenon.

Partial rivalry is usually couched in terms of a cost measured in the numeraire, and as such, Tinbergen's approach couched in terms of consumption units has sparked little interest. Furthermore, the policy relevance of this distinction seems largely absent. Perhaps because the sole motivation for the distinction is notational convenience, Tinbergen fails to give convincing illustrative examples or applications.

8. Crowded or congested public goods are often seen to fill the mid-range between public and private goods.[9] For example, Oakland [1972] shows diagrammatically how private goods become completely crowded at a quantity of one, public goods never get crowded and mixed goods suffer increasing crowding costs with increasing use.

Two things detract from the generality of viewing congestion costs as the measure through which mixed goods can be defined. First, the cost of crowding usually takes on the nature of an external cost imposed on other users. In general, however, the cost associated with more people using a good could be a resource production cost, an extra maintenance cost, an external cost or any other kind of cost. Second, often what would be the uncrowded public good becomes solely a vehicle for congestion reduction. This makes the mixed goods case basically a capacity choice model in a private good model with an external congestion cost. Indeed, from the point of view of the congestion models there would be no reason to increase the public good if it were not crowded, whereas from the public goods perspective, more units of the public good, even if the existing units are uncrowded, are still valued by consumers.

This second point can be illustrated by an example that will also serve to set the stage for 12. Consider a crowdable bridge. Two dimensions will be relevant, the number of cars crossing the bridge and the number of lanes. The number of lanes is like a public good in the sense of 4 in that all drivers consume (in the sense of having access to) the same lanes. The number of cars crossing the bridge is like a private good in that the benefit of a single car crossing accrues privately to the occupants of the car. If consumers get no utility directly from lanes, then the addition of lanes is efficacious only because it increases the bridge's capacity to produce crossings. For a never crowded bridge, one lane is all that is required. In such a case we really have a private good/capacity choice model. Alternatively, consumers may get utility directly from the lanes themselves. In this case, even after the value of the lanes in capacity enhancement is calculated in terms of congestion reduction, we must still consider the pure value of the lanes themselves. This value will be measurable in terms of a summation of MRSs for lanes.

Policy-wise, crowding can turn non-rival goods into rival goods. This would seem to indicate that the continuum of mixed goods takes on the character of private goods at least in the sense of rival consumption. The pure public good is now the "knife edge" polar case with all other goods characterized by a greater or lesser degree of congestion. This approach leads to a laissez faire conclusion for all but what must be considered unusual cases of non-crowdable public goods. This tidy free market directive can be challenged, however, by asserting that the crowding cost takes the nature of an external cost.[10] In this case, however, the motivation for public sector involvement would come from externalities and not from public goods.

9. Another common theme is that ranges of positive externality explain the distinction between public and private goods.[11] If the externality is universal, then the notational analysis of it will be similar to that of a pure public good. For example, if my consumption or production activity affects the utility of every person in the society, then in assessing costs and

benefits we would have to count everyone's MRS for the activity. The marginal equalities in this case will involve the familiar summation of MRSs. If there were no externalities, then all goods would be private. Incomplete externalities give rise to mixed goods. It is evident that 4 and 6 can be motivated by this externality issue. Clubs may form precisely because of reciprocal externalities in the small group.

It is also clear that the externalities view masks the underlying influence of the issues of exclusion costs and non-rival consumption. With costless exclusion, there would not be any "external" benefits bestowed on third parties. Non payers could be excluded from enjoying the benefits, meanwhile any user's payment (or potential user's offer of payment) effectively internalizes the benefits to the original actor's decision making process. However, note that regardless of the exclusion issue, the non-rival consumption aspect of positive externalities (that is simultaneous consumption by more than one person) still requires the marginal equalities describing optimality to use the summation of MRSs clearly, for there to be a positive externality requires the inability to exclude non-payers, but the summation of MRSs is required whenever consumption is non-rival. Therefore, implicitly, those that liken public goods to externalities are using both the non-excludability and non-rivalry aspects in their definition of public goods. This is perhaps, the most common position, but it does have the drawback of unnecessarily combining two separable aspects, and in so doing, losing some of the richness and variety that comes from keeping rivalry and excludability separate.

The similarity between public goods and externalities does lead some to draw conclusions about the normative issue of whether the public good should be produced publicly or privately. The argument usually goes as follows. Since we know that the public sector has a role to play in correcting externalities through Pigouvian tax/subsidy schemes, and since public goods are like extenalities, it therefore follows that the public sector has a role to play in public good provision. However, one might just as easily argue along the following lines. Since Coase demonstrated that the private sector does have the correct incentives with respect to dealing with and internalizing externalities, the public sector has no role to play in correcting externalities and, therefore, no role in public good provision either.

The preceding argument illustrates this paper's theme nicely. Free market economists build up from the private good case with no externalities to achieve efficient production of mixed goods through Coasian internalization of what would be externalities. Alternatively, the market interventionist position draws sharp parallels between public sector correction of externalities and public sector involvement in public good production.

10. As evidenced above, excludability is an important issue in the discussion of the connection between public goods and externalities. But it is a different factor than non-rivalry and separable from non-rivalry. The models of excludable non-rival goods in footnote 3 clearly show this. Actually, it is curious that the issue of excludability gained prominence in conjunction with the non-rival aspect in Samuelson's [1954] treatment. This is because non-excludability seems a much more crucial problem for rival goods than for non-rival goods. If a rival good was non-excludable it is doubtful whether the private sector would ever produce any. Firms would not build cars if anyone could just drive them away without paying. Neither would an individual build his own car if, because of non-excludability, he could not guarantee that he would be able to use it. Meanwhile, for non-rival goods, production may not be optimal, but it will not be zero. As the models of voluntary provision of public goods (footnote 8) point out, each person is at least guaranteed that he will be able to consume his own production.

In trying to flesh out the mixed good case there are at least two possibilities. The first would be to conclude that almost all goods are subject to partial or costly exclusion. Indeed, automobiles, which are usually considered to be pure private goods, must be equipped, at a cost, with locking devices to guarantee the exclusion of non-payers. At the other end of the spectrum, national defense could be made excludable, for a cost. It appears that economists have been sloppy in their usage of non-excludability. There are always costs of exclusion and when economists invoke non-excludability they implicitly mean that the costs of exclusion are not worth the benefits. When economists analyze an excludable good they implicitly mean that the exclusion costs are low enough to be incurred.

According to this first distinction, all goods are, potentially, mixed goods. This realization provides the point of view for Staaf's position in 3, where the magnitude of the costs and benefits of exclusion will determine whether the goods will be excludable or non-excludable. Coming to the mixed goods case from the direction of private (in the sense of excludable) goods, one focuses attention on the institutions that spontaneously develop to introduce or enhance excludability; institutions like fences, locks and legal enforcement, or community acceptance, of private property rights. If one instead came to mixed goods from the direction of public (in the sense of non-excludable) goods, then one would focus attention on the public expenditure and public finance issues highlighted by Samuelson [1954], the public choice issues championed by Buchanan, and to a lesser extent, the cost savings from relaxing excludability.

The second possible interpretation of the exclusion criterion is to eliminate the middle ground altogether, sliding all goods to the private, excludable, pole. As made explicit by Tyler Cowen [1985] and implicitly underlying Borcherding's [1978] arguments, all goods are perfectly excludable simply by not producing another unit. At the optimal margin the summation of MRSs must equal the marginal cost. Unless all individuals with positive MRSs agree to pay, the marginal unit will not be produced. On the inframarginal units there are incentives for bluffing and free riding but at the margin, which for allocative efficiency is where it counts, exclusion is perfect. In this sense, all goods are excludable and private, and the invisible hand reigns.

11. One of the curious distinctions between public and private goods involves the marginal cost of allowing additional consumers to enjoy the good. For a public good this cost is zero. For a private good this cost is positive. Apparently, there is no middle range in this instance.

It is important to note that exclusion takes on a different meaning here, one with normative consequences. Exclusion is the act of preventing someone from consuming a good. Excludability, as considered in 3 and 10, is a descriptive or defining aspect of the private good. Here, however, even if non-payers could be excluded costlessly, there should be no exclusion on the margin if marginal cost is zero. Anyone with a positive MRS should be allowed to consume the "free" good in order to obtain Pareto optimal distribution.

Notwithstanding the zero marginal cost of additional users, the public good must be produced and this production will be costly. With respect to allowing more individuals to consume the good, this cost takes the form of an overhead cost.[12] The combination of an overhead cost and a constant per unit variable cost, be it zero or positive, is reminiscent of decreasing cost or natural monopoly models. Indeed, several authors have been led to conclude that the public good represents a special case of extreme decreasing cost.[13] These authors are not constructing the mixed goods case from the pure polar cases, rather they are extending and analogizing from the private good topic of decreasing cost to a limiting case, i.e. zero marginal cost. With this viewpoint pure public goods have zero marginal cost, mixed goods have positive marginal cost but decreasing average cost, and pure private goods have constant or increasing average cost.

Once again the policy conclusions associated with this point of view depend on one's perspective. For example, Samuelson [1955, p.356] himself argued that "Governments provide or regulate services that are incapable of being produced under the strict conditions of constant returns." Presumably, therefore, government has a role to play in public goods since the public good can be likened to a limiting case of a decreasing cost industry. To counter this interventionist position, however, Demsetz [1968] argues that, because of competition for the market, decreasing costs do not cause market failure. Also, price discrimination and various forms of nonlinear pricing allow firms with decreasing cost to recoup their overhead costs with lump sum charges, while at the same time having the initiative to set the per unit price on the margin equal to marginal cost, thereby achieving socially optimal distribution. Furthermore, when competition between decreasing cost sellers is considered, there is pressure to bring about this nice welfare result. See Shmanske [1991b]. In these views, private sector public good provision could certainly be possible.

12. The discussions of crowding cost and zero marginal cost both hinted that there are actually two dimensions of consumption relevant in public goods analysis. This is the view presented in Shmanske [1982] and further developed by Else [1988] and Shmanske [1990], [1991a]. In one dimension consumption is rival and in another dimension consumption is non-rival. These dimensions are called the utilization dimension and the public good dimension. Since consumption is rival in the utilization

dimension, this dimension looks just like a standard private good where the MRS is set equal to marginal cost and demands are summed horizontally. The non-rival consumption in the other dimension makes it look like a pure public good dimension in which MRSs are added together for comparison with marginal cost and demands are summed vertically.

In the pure public good case, the private-like dimension becomes trivial and is dropped from the analysis. Indeed, it makes little sense to define different individual consumption measures for national defense. Everyone utilizes national defense once each time period. Therefore, only the non-rival public good dimension remains in the pure public good case. Likewise, in the pure private good case, the public good dimension is trivial and dropped from consideration. For example, if the quality of a good is immutable for some reason, so that all individuals consume the same given quality, as in standard textbook private good models, then there is no economic choice in that dimension and all emphasis will be only on each individual's different utilization level.

For the continuum of mixed goods both dimensions are important. A good example is a park. The public good dimension is the acreage of the park, which is non-rival and to which all individuals have access. Vertical summations of MRSs in this dimension are relevant. The utilization dimension measures the number of visits to the park. In this dimension optimality requires that each user's MRS must be equal to the marginal cost. This marginal cost may be zero or close to zero in some cases, but it also may be sharply rising. Demand curves are summed horizontally in the utilization dimension just like a normal private good.

The mixed good is truly a mixture or combination of the two separate dimensions. In this view the mixed good is the general case and the pure polar cases are simplifications that lack a certain dimensionality. Policy-wise, we are led to consider the same issues as in many of the other formulations. Recognizing that the mixed good has a rival dimension, can private producers price and exclude in this dimension to optimally supply the correct amount of the good in two dimensions or, recognizing the non-rival dimension, do market institutions fail to adequately capture costs and benefits in this dimension? Policy conclusions follow from whichever dimension is emphasized.

13. The notions of rival and non-rival consumption are usually emphasized in discussions of public goods. Indeed, it is this basic notion of non-rivalry

that Samuelson originally captured mathematically. Many of the above distinctions are derivatives of the basic difference between rival and non-rival consumption.

While at first it must seem that there is no middle ground - consumption is either rival or non-rival - in fact, three interesting middle grounds have been examined. First, types of partial rivalry were discussed in 7, 8, and 11. For 8, the partial rivalry is due to a crowding cost associated with more consumption. In 7, Tinbergen captures the partial rivalry in the same dimension as the consumption. Meanwhile, in 11, the partial rivalry is captured most generally as any type of extra production cost in a decreasing cost situation.

The second type of middle ground developed a different kind of partial rivalry in 4 and 6. In these cases, non-rival consumption was not universal, it only spread to a subset of consumers. These cases are best known as the theory of clubs.

Finally, a third type of mixed good was hinted at in 5 and made explicit in 12. The good in question must simultaneously have rival consumption characteristics and non-rival consumption characteristics to be considered a mixed good. In 5, this leads to both vertical and horizontal summations in a diagrammatic analysis. In 12, it is emphasized that the horizontal and vertical summations must be taken in different dimensions.

All of these cases have illustrated the theme of the paper. When the non-rival or public attributes are emphasized in the mixed good, the usual simple market solutions that work for pure private goods are inadequate to properly equate costs and benefits at the margin. Alternatively, when the private or rival characteristics are emphasized in the mixed good, attention is drawn to more sophisticated free market institutions and the entrepreneurial ingenuity that will bring this about. In this view, the market does properly capture marginal costs and benefits.

Summary

As the abundance of references illustrates, these topics have been presented before. The contribution of this paper is to gather the many threads in this disparate literature together in one place, addressing one theme. The tone of the paper is conciliatory rather than combative -the goal being to show the connections between the different threads and to show the implications of following any one particular thread, rather than arguing in favor of one viewpoint over another. Several messages stand out. First, there are many different characteristics that one could employ to separate public goods from private goods. Second, for most of these cases the goods in the real world must be considered as mixed rather than at on or the other of the poles. Third, in many cases the policy conclusions associated with any one type of mixed good are still ambiguous, depending on whether the private attributes or the public attributes are emphasized in the mixture.

Therefore, in recognition of these three messages, we must all exercise extreme care in referring to public or mixed goods because the term is vague enough to be used in different settings with widely different policy implications. Cavalier reference to public goods, such as the overused rhetoric that something is "like a public good," without an explicit statement of what is comprehended and implied in the phrase, is likely to lead to confusion and disagreement, and should be avoided.

References

Auster, Richard D., "Private Markets in Public Goods (or Qualities)," Quarterly Journal of Economics, Vol.91, No. 3, (Aug.1977) pp.419-30.

Berglas, Eitan and David Pines, "Club, Local Public Goods and Transportation Models: A Synthesis," Journal of Public Economics, Vol. 15, (1981) pp. 141-62.

Bergstrom, Theodore, Lawrence Blume and Hal Varian, "On the Private Provision of Public Goods," Journal of Public Economics, Vol.29, No. 1, (Feb. 1986), pp. 25-49.

Blair, Roger D. and Lawrence W. Kenny, Microeconomics with Business Applications, John Wiley & Sons, New York, 1987.

Bliss, Christopher and Barry Nalebuff, "Dragon-Slaying and Ballroom Dancing: The Private Supply of a Public Good," Journal of Public Economics, Vol.25, No. 1, (Nov. 1984) pp. 1-12.

Borcherding, Thomas E., "Competition, Exclusion and the Optimal Supply of Public Goods," The Journal of Law and Economics, Vol.21, No. 2, (Apr. 1978) pp. 111-32.

Boyd, J. Hayden, "Joint Products, Collective Goods and External Effects: Comment " Journal of Political Economy, Vol.79, No. 5, (Sept.1971) pp. 1138-40.

Brennan, Geoffrey and Cliff Walsh, "A Monopoly Model of Public Goods Provision: The Uniform Pricing Case," American Economic Review, Vol. 71, No. 1, (March 1981) pp. 196-206.

Brennan, Geoffrey and Cliff Walsh, "Private Markets in (Excludable) Public Goods: A Reexamination," Quarterly Journal of Economics, Vol.100, No. 3, (Aug. 1985) pp. 811-19.

Brito, Dagobert L. and William H. Oakland, "On the Monopolistic Provision of Excludable Public Goods," American Economic Review, Vol.70, No. 4, (Sept. 1980) pp. 691-704.

Browning, Edgar K. and Jacquelene M. Browning, Microeconomic Theory and Applications 2nd, Little, Brown and Company, Boston, 1986.

Buchanan, James H., "An Economic Theory of Clubs," Economica, Vol.32, No. 125, (Feb. 1965) pp. 1-14.

Buchanan, James H., "Joint supply, Externality and Optimality," Economica, Vol. 33, No. 132, (Nov. 1966) pp. 404-15.

Buchanan, James M., The Demand and Supply of Public Goods, (Rand McNally & Company, Chicago), 1968.

Buchanan, James M. and Milton F. Kaflogis, "A Note on Public Goods Supply," American Economic Review, Vol. 53, No. 3, (June 1963) pp. 403-14.

Burns, Michael E. and Cliff Walsh, "Market Provision of Price-Excludable Public Goods: A General Analysis," Journal of Political Economy, Vol. 89, No. 1, (Feb. 1981) pp. 166-91.

Call, Steven T. and William L. Holahan, Microeconomics Wadsworth Publishing Company, Belmont, CA, 1980.

Christainsen, Gregory B., "Evidence for Determining the Optimal Mechanism for Providing Collective Goods," American Economist, Vol.26, No, 1 (Spring 1982) pp. 57-61.

Coase, Ronald, "The Problem of Social Cost," The Journal of Law and Economics, Vol. 3, No. 2, (Oct. 1960) pp. 1-44.

Collinge, R. A., "Toward 'Privatization' of Public Sector Output: Decentralized Contracting for Public and Private Goods," Journal of Public Economics, Vol. 27, No. 3, (Aug.   1985) pp. 371-87.

Cornes, Richard and Todd Sandler, "Easy Riders, Joint Production and Public Goods," Economic Journal, Vol. 94, No. 375, (Sept. 1984a) pp. 580-98.

Cornes, Richard and Todd Sandler, "On the Consistency of Conjectures with Public Goods," Journal of Public Economics, Vol.27, No.1, (June 1985a) pp. 125-9.

Cornes, Richard and Todd Sandler, "The Simple Analytics of Pure Public Good Provision," Economica, Vol. 52, No. 105, (Feb. 1985b) pp. 103-16.

Cornes, Richard and Todd Sandler, "The Theory of Public Goods: Non-Nash Behavior," Journal of Public Economics, Vol.23, No.3, (Apr. 1984a) pp.367-79.

Cowen, Tyler, "Public Goods Definitions and Their Institutional Content: A Critique of Public Goods Theory," Review of Social Economy, Vol.43, No. 1, (Apr. 1985) pp. 53-63.

Davis, Otto A. and Andrew B. Whinston, "On the Distinction Between Public and Private Goods," American Economic Review, Vol.57, No.2, (May 1967) pp. 360-73.

Demsetz, Harold, "Joint Supply and Price Discrimination," The Journal of Law and Economics, Vol. 16, No. 2, (Oct. 1973a) pp. 389-405.

Demsetz, Harold, "Reply to Professor Thompson," The Journal of Law and Economics, Vol. 16, No. 2, (Oct. 1973b) pp. 413-15.

Demsetz, Harold, "The Private Production of Public Goods," The Journal of Law and Economics, Vol. 13, No. 2, (Oct. 1970) pp. 293-306.

Demsetz, Harold, "Why Regulate Utilities?," The Journal of Law and Economics, Vol. 11, No. 1, (Apr. 1968) pp. 55-65.

DeSerpa, Allan C., "Congestion, Pollution and Impure Public Goods," Public Finance, Vol. 33, No. 1-2, (1978) pp. 68-83.

DeSerpa, Allan C., Microeconomic Theory: Issues and Applications, Allyn and Bacon, Inc., Boston, 1985.

Dorfman, Robert, "On Optimal Congestion," Journal of Environmental Economics and Management Vol.11, No.2, (June 1984) pp. 91-106.

Eaton, B. Curtis and Diane F. Eaton, Microeconomics, W. H. Freeman and Company, New York, 1988.

Ekelund, Robert B., "The Fragile Nature of Public Goods Equilibria," Review of Social Economy, Vol. 35, No. 3, (Oct. 1977) pp. 204-11.

Else, Peter K., "Further Thoughts on Public Goods, Private Goods and Mixed Goods," Scottish Journal of Political Economy, Vol.35, No.2, (May 1988) pp. 115-128.

Evans, Alan W., "Private Good, Externality, Public Good," Scottish Journal of Political Economy, Vol. 22, No. 1, (Feb. 1970) pp. 79-89.

Friedman, David D., Price Theory: An Intermediate Text South Western Publishing Co., Livermore, CA, 1986.

Head, John G., "Mixed Goods in Samuelson Geometry," Public Finance, Vol.31, No. 3, (1976) pp. 313-39.

Head, John G., "Public Goods and Public Policy," Public Finance, Vol.17, No. 3, (1962) pp. 197-219.

Head, John G. and Carl S. Shoup, "Public Goods, Private Goods and Ambiguous Goods," The Economic Journal, Vol. 79, No. 315, (Sept. 1969) pp. 567-72.

Hemenway, David, Prices and Choices 2nd, Ballinger Publishing Co., Cambridge, Mass., 1988.

Hirshleifer, Jack, "From Weakest-Link to Best Shot: The Voluntary Provision of Public Goods," Public Choice, Vol. 41, No. 1, (1983) pp. 371-86.

Hirshleifer, Jack, Price Theory and Applications 4th, Prentice Hall, Englewood Cliffs, NJ, 1988.

Holtermann, S. E., "Externalities and Public Goods," Economica, Vol.39, No. 153, (Feb. 1972) pp. 78-87.

Hyman, David N., Modern Microeconomics: Analysis and Applications, Times Mirror/Mosby College Publishing, St. Louis, 1986.

James, Estelle, "Joint Products, Collective Goods, and External Effects: Comments", Journal of Political Economy Vol.79, No.5, (Sept.1971) pp. 1127-35.

Katzner, Donald W., Walrasian Economics: An Introduction to the Economic Theory of Market Behavior, Addison Wesley Publishing Co., Menlo Park, CA, 1988.

Kohler, Heinz, Intermediate Microeconomics: Theory and Applications 2nd, Scott, Foresman and Company, Glenview, Ill., 1986.

Laux-Meiselbach, "Impossibility of Exclusion and Characteristics of Public Goods," Journal of Public Economics, Vol.36, No.1, (June 1988) pp. 127-37.

Lerner, Abba P., "Conflicting Principles of Public Utility Price Regulation," The Journal of Law and Economics, Vol.7, No.2, (Oct. 1964) pp. 61-70.

Mansfield, Edwin, Microeconomics: Theory and Applications 5th, W. W. Norton & Company, New York, 1985.

McCloskey, Donald N., The Applied Theory of Price 2nd, MacMillan Publishing Co., New York, 1985.

McGuire, Martin C. and Carl H. Groth, Jr., "A Method for Identifying the Public Good Allocation Process Within a Group," Quarterly Journal of Economics, Vol. 100, No. 5, (Supp. 1985) pp. 915-34.

Minasian, Jora R., "Television Pricing and the Theory of Public Goods " The Journal of Law and Economics, Vol.7, No.2, (Oct. 1964) pp.71-80.

Mishan, E. J., "Joint Product, Collective Goods, and External Effects. Reply," Journal of Political Economy, Vol.79, No.5, (Sept. 1971a) pp.1141-50.

Mishan, E. J., "The Postwar Literature on Externalities: An Interpretive Essay," Journal of Economic Literature, Vol.9, No.1, (Mar. 1971b) pp. 1-28.

Mishan, E. J., "The Relationship Between Joint Products, Collective Goods, and External Effects," Journal of Political Economy, Vol.77, No.3, (May 1969) pp. 329-49.

Muzondo, Timothy, "Mixed and Pure Public Goods, User Charges, and Welfare," Public Finance, Vol. 33, No. 3, (1978) pp. 314-30.

Oakland, William H., "Congestion, Public Goods and Welfare," Journal of Public Economics, Vol. 1, (1972) pp. 339-57.

Oakland, William H., "Public Goods, Perfect Competition, and Underproduction," Journal of Political Economy, Vol.82, No.5, (Sept. 1974) pp. 927-39.

Olson, Mancur Jr. and Richard Zeckhauser, "The Efficient Production of External Economies," American Economic Review, Vol.60, No.3, (June 1970) pp. 512-7.

Samuelson, Paul A., "Aspects of Public Expenditure Theories," The Review of Economics and Statistics, Vol.40, No.4, (Nov.1958) pp. 332-8.

Samuelson, Paul A., "Diagrammatic Exposition of a Theory of Public Expenditure," The Review of Economics and Statistics, Vol.37, No.4, (Nov. 1955) pp. 350-6.

Samuelson, Paul A., "Public Goods and Subscription TV: A Correction of the Record," The Journal of Law and Economics, Vol.7, No.2, (Oct.1964) pp. 81-3.

Samuelson, Paul A., "The Pure Theory of Public Expenditure," The Review of Economics and Statistics, Vol. 36, No.4, (Nov.1954) pp. 387-9.

Samuelson, Paul A., "Pure Theory of Public Expenditure and Taxation," in Public Economics, ed. by J. Margolis and H. Guitton, MacMillan and Co. Ltd., (London, 1969).

Sandler, Todd, "Pareto Optimality, Pure Public Goods, Impure Public Goods and Multiregional Spillovers," Scottish Journal of Political Economy, Vol. 22, No. 1, (Feb. 1975) pp. 25-38.

Sandler, Todd and John T. Tschirart, "Mixed Clubs: Further Observations," Journal of Public Economics, Vol. 23, (1984) pp. 381-9.

Shmanske, Stephen, "A Note on Else's Treatment of Quality and Public Goods," Scottish Journal of Political Economy, Vol. 37, No.2, (May 1990) pp.193-6.

Shmanske, Stephen, "News as a Public Good: Cooperative Ownership, Price Commitments, and the Success of the Associated Press," Business History Review, Vol. 60, (Spring 1986) pp. 55-80.

Shmanske, Stephen, Public Goods. Mixed Goods, and Monopolistic Competition, Texas A&M University Press, (College Station, Texas, 1991a).

Shmanske, Stephen, "Public Goods, Product Quality Determination and Dimensionality of Consumption," Public Finance, Vol.37, No.3, (Fall 1982), pp. 387-403.

Shmanske, Stephen, "Two Part Pricing in Differentiated Duopoly," Journal of Institutional and Theoretical Economics, Vol.147, No.3, (Sept. 1991b) pp. 441-58.

Singer, Neil, H., "Joint Products, Collective Goods, and External Effects: Comment," Journal of Political Economy, Vol.79, No.5, (Sept.1971) pp.1136-7.

Staaf, Robert J., "Privatization of Public Goods," Public Choice, Vol.41, No. 3, (1983) pp. 435-40.

Sugden, R., "Reciprocity: The Supply of Public Goods Through Voluntary Contributions," Economic Journal, Vol.94, No. 376, (Dec. 1984) pp.772-87.

Thompson, Earl A., "A Note on Consumer-Producer Collusion in the Private Marketing of Collective-Type Goods," Discussion Paper #142, Department of Economics, University of California, Los Angeles, (Jan.1979).

Thompson, Earl A., "The Perfectly Competitive Production of Collective Goods," The Review of Economics and Statistics, Vol.50, No.1, (Feb. 1968) pp. 1-12.

Thompson, Earl A., "The Private Production of Public Goods: A Comment," The Journal of Law and Economics, Vol. 16, No.2, (Oct. 1973) pp.407-12.

Tinbergen, Jan, "On Collective and Part-Collective Goods," De Economist, Vol. 12, No. 2, (1984) pp. 171-82.

Varian, Hal R., Intermediate Microeconomics: A Modern Approach, W. W. Norton & Company, New York, 1987.

Walsh, Cliff, "A Reconsideration of Some Aspects of the Private Production of Public Goods," Review of Social Economy, Vol.39, No.1, (Apr.1981) pp. 19-35.

NOTES

1. Six of the texts (Blair and Kenny [1987], Browning and Browning 1986], Eaton and Eaton [1988], Hemenway [1988], Hyman [1986], and Kohler [1986]) identify both non-rivalry and non-excludability as defining public goods. Four texts (Call and Holahan [1980], Hirshleifer [1988], Katzner [1988], and Mansfield [1985]) identify only the non-rivalry aspect as the distinguishing feature of public goods. The four remaining texts have still different views on what constitutes a public good. McCloskey 1985] mentions public goods but does not either dwell on them or define them. Friedman [1986] defines public goods with only the non-excludability characteristic.   Deserpa [1985] highlights three characteristics: non-rivalry, non-excludability and indivisibility.   Finally, Varian [1987] defines public goods as these for which all must consume the same amount.

2. Actually the causality may run the other way. That is, an economist may choose a particular definition because it leads to a particular policy conclusion that for normative reasons the economist thinks is proper. This paper is primarily interested in the logical connection between the definition and the policy conclusions and not the strategic choice of definitions.   However, given that the choice of definitions will affect outcomes, I invite the reader to speculate as to why different economists choose different definitions.

3. There are several different versions of private sector, public (in the sense of non-rival) good production. The conclusions of these models run the gamut from underproduction through optimal production to overproduction. See Auster [1977], Borcherding [1978], Brennan and Walsh [1981], [1985], Brito and Oakland [1980], Burns and Walsh [1981], Demsetz [1970], 1973a], [1973b], Ekelund [1977] Minasian [1964], Oakland [1974], Samuelson [1964], Shmanske [1982], [1986], [1990], 1991a], Thompson [1968], [1973], [1979], and Walsh [1981].

4. Samuelson [1969b] p. 108.

5. The use of national defense as an example also masks another issue that is discussed in 12.

6. The extra constraint might not really be extra if the cost conditions evidenced some joint cost or other form of non-rival consumption such that the private good formulation would also lead to identical consumption for each individual.   Barring the exclusion costs to be considered below, the utilities that are achieved might then be equal between the public good formulation and the private good formulation.

7. By bringing in issues of excludability here, Staaf reveals that the issue of quantity adjustment by the consumer stems from the more basic notion of excludability.

8. There is an abundant literature on the voluntary provision of public goods.   See Bergstrom, Blume and Varian [1986], Bliss and Nalebuff [1984], Christainsen [1982], Cornes and Sandler [1984a], [1984b], [1985a], [1985b], Hirshleifer [1983], McGuire and Groth [1985] and Sugden [1984].

9. See Berglas and Pines [1981], Deserpa [1978], Dorfman [1984], Muzondo [1978], Oakland [1972], Sandler [1975], and Sandler and Tschirart [1984].

10. Note that this differs from the discussion of ranges of externality that is considered next in 9.   There we will consider ranges of external benefits whereas the congestion cost is an external cost.

11. See Boyd [1971], Buchanan [1966], [1968], Buchanan and Kaflogis [1963], Evans [1970], Head [1976], Holtermann [1972], James [1971], Mishan [1969],[1971a], [197lb], and Olson and Zeckhauser [1970).

12. Sometimes the term "fixed cost" is used carelessly when the notion of overhead cost is meant. This should be avoided.   An overhead cost does not vary with output except at the quantity zero. A fixed cost does not vary in the short run but becomes variable in the long run.   Some writers have been led to conclude that a good may be a private good in the short run because of the potentially rival (although not rival because of zero marginal cost) consumption and because of the marginal equalities that have each person's MRS equal to zero.   Meanwhile, the good is a public good in the long run as the   of "fixed" cost is varied to supply more of the non-rival good.   See Mishan [197lb] and Singer [1971].   There are, in fact, two dimensions of production, one which leads to rival consumption and one which leads to non-rival consumption.   However, what is called a fixed cost is actually an overhead cost in the rival dimension and a variable cost

n the non-rival dimension. It exists simultaneously in both dimensions in both the long and short run and can be varied in both the long and short un. Consequently, fixed costs and fixed factors have nothing to do with the analysis.

Mishan and Singer were struggling with the idea of two dimensions of production and consumption but obscured their analysis by inappropriate use of the language of fixed and variable, long run and short run. An appropriate language was developed in Shmanske [1982] and is discussed n the next section.

3. For examples see Davis and Whinston [1967), Head [1962], Lerner 1964], and Samuelson [1955], [1958], [1969]. For criticism and further explanation see Shmanske [1982] and [1991a].